Robert Louis Stevenson

YOUNG STORYTELLER

Robert Louis Stevenson

YOUNG STORYTELLER

by Francene Sabin
illustrated by Pamela Johnson

Troll Associates

Library of Congress Cataloging-in-Publication Data

Sabin, Francene.
    Robert Louis Stevenson: young storyteller / by Francene Sabin;
illustrated by Pamela Johnson.
        p.   cm.
    Summary: Describes the life of the Scottish author who endured a
sickly childhood and produced many popular novels and poems.
    ISBN 0-8167-2507-1 (lib. bdg.)   ISBN 0-8167-2508-X (pbk.)
    1. Stevenson, Robert Louis, 1850-1894—Biography—Youth—Juvenile
literature.   2. Authors, Scottish—19th century—Biography—Juvenile
literature.   [1. Stevenson, Robert Louis, 1850-1894.   2. Authors,
Scottish.]   I. Johnson, Pamela, ill.   II. Title.
PR5493.S23   1992
828'.809—dc20
    [B]   91-3924

Copyright © 1992 by Troll Associates.

Printed in the United States of America.

10   9   8   7   6   5   4   3   2   1

Robert Louis Stevenson

YOUNG STORYTELLER

The little boy lay shivering in the dark. Like many children, Lou saw scary things in the shadowy corners of his room. He knew the monsters weren't real. They were never there in the daylight. They were never there when his parents or Mrs. Cunningham, his nursemaid, came into the room. But when Lou was alone in the dark, the scary things were very real.

Young Robert Louis Stevenson, called Lou by his family, often cried at bedtime. Bedtime meant the dark of night, when the shadows came to life. Every evening, Lou begged Mrs. Cunningham not to leave him alone. One night, she had an idea.

"Come here, to the window," Cummy said. Cummy was the boy's nickname for his nurse. "Look outside. Do you see the lampposts all along the street? Now just wait a moment. Something wonderful is going to happen."

The boy and his nurse sat in silence. He clutched her hand and shivered. A cold wind blew down the street. It made leaves dance and tree branches creak and crack.

"See...he is coming now."

Lou gazed hard into the gloomy street. He saw a man moving slowly from lamppost to lamppost. The man carried an oil lantern in his left hand. Its flame flickered as he walked. He carried a short ladder over his right shoulder.

The man stopped at each lamppost and set down the ladder. Then he climbed the ladder to a glass box at the top of the post. He opened one side of the box and leaned his lantern into it. Like magic, a flame glowed inside the box. The man closed the glass door, climbed down, and moved on to the next lamppost.

"Cummy," Lou whispered, "is that how the stars in the sky are lighted every night?"

The gray-haired woman smiled and stroked the boy's dark hair. "That's a lovely thought. What a fine story it would make." Then she pointed at the lamppost right in front of the Stevenson house. "Watch closely. Leerie is going to light a star just for you!"

As the little boy stared through the window, Mrs. Cunningham talked on in a calm, kind voice. She said, "Any time you can't sleep, or when you wake from a bad dream, just think about your own star. Every night it will glow close by. It will make your room safe," she promised.

Lou nodded. He was sure the light would work the way Cummy promised. He hoped it would keep the scary things away.

Years later, Robert Louis Stevenson remembered how he had felt as a little boy in the darkness. In *A Child's Garden of Verses,* he wrote:

"For we are very lucky, with a lamp before the door,
And Leerie stops to light it as he lights so many more;
And oh! before you hurry by with ladder and with light,
Oh Leerie, see a little child and nod to him tonight!"

The grown-up Stevenson was famous for his poems. He was also famous for his adventure stories. He had a marvelous imagination. He wrote about pirates, brave soldiers, daring heroes, murder, and monsters. In his poems, he told of faraway places, of nature, of the Scottish Highlands, of Pacific islands, of ships roaming the seas, and of childhood memories.

Stevenson's ideas came partly from his travels as a grownup. But mostly they came from a world he imagined when he was a child. Young Lou needed his made-up world to fill many lonely days and nights in his room.

Lou was very sick for much of his childhood. From the time he was born, on November 13, 1850, in Edinburgh, Scotland, the boy was in poor health. His parents loved him very much and did all they could to help him.

Lou's mother, Margaret, was a lively, warm woman. She had a fine imagination and a wonderful sense of humor. And she understood how it felt to be sick. Like her son, she was forced to stay in bed for many months at a time.

Today we know that Lou, his mother, and other members of the Stevenson family had a disease called tuberculosis. Nowadays, tuberculosis is cured by medicines called antibiotics. But when the Stevensons lived, there was no cure for this disease. People didn't even know what caused it. The most common way to treat tuberculosis was with bed rest.

In the nineteenth century, tuberculosis was a lifetime illness. People sometimes got better for a while. But sooner or later they became sick again. During the bad times, they were too weak and feverish to lead a normal life.

Sickness ruled little Lou's childhood. During his long months in bed he passed the dreary hours playing in a make-believe world. His bed became the "Land of Counterpane." Counterpane is an old-fashioned word for "bedspread."

On some days, Lou's bed became a battlefield. Tin soldiers marched across the covers to fight bitter wars against other armies. Behind the mountains formed by Lou's knees there were cities of gold and silver. Dragons and knights and wizards lived in dark woods. Pirate ships sailed on the wrinkled woolen seas, passing uncharted islands. Many hours were spent this way and many stories filled the boy's mind.

Lou also liked it when his mother read her
favorite stories to him. One of these was the play
Macbeth by William Shakespeare. It tells of
Scottish chieftains, witches, ghosts, murders, and
revenge. Lou found *Macbeth* very scary, but he
looked forward eagerly to each day's reading.

Lou's father had a different way of amusing his
sick son. Thomas Stevenson was an engineer and
inventor. He was a quiet, serious man. But he had
an offbeat sense of humor, and he used it to help
Lou over the bad times.

17

Mr. Stevenson sometimes sat in a chair just outside Lou's door, acting out stories. He used just his voice to play different roles as he pretended to talk to make-believe characters.

Sometimes the conversations were funny, like the time when Mr. Stevenson chatted with two dogs that lived in a nearby house. Sometimes Lou heard the voices of a sailor and his parrot, or a shepherdess living in the Highlands who was always losing her sheep. Every character had a long, colorful conversation with Lou's father.

Mr. Stevenson was a very patient man. He kept on talking well into the night. He didn't stop until he knew his restless son was asleep.

Lou did not go to school until he was almost seven years old. And he was not taught to read until then. The Stevensons were not worried about this. Lou was a bright boy. He learned many things without reading about them. He liked to draw and paint. He also made up stories. Then his mother wrote them down and Lou drew pictures to go with the stories.

In 1856, when Lou was six, an uncle held a contest among all of the children in the family. The winner was to get a gold coin. The children had to write out the story of Moses from the Bible, using their own words. Lou didn't know how to write. So he told the story in drawings. They showed the followers of Moses wearing top hats, carrying umbrellas, and wearing rubber boots as they crossed the Red Sea. Lou won the prize for his funny, clever drawings.

Mr. and Mrs. Stevenson were wise not to worry about their son's education. Lou learned to read as soon as he started school. He began writing soon after that. And once he began to write, he didn't stop putting his ideas on paper for the rest of his life.

Lou had a hard time at his first school. He was not like the other children in his class. He did not know all the games they played. He did not know the slang words everyone else used. He talked like a little grownup, and he dressed the same way.

Worst of all, Cummy walked Lou to school every morning, and came to take him home every afternoon. She made sure he walked under her umbrella. She insisted that he wear rubber boots, even when there was hardly any rain.

Worrying about Lou's health made sense to Cummy and the Stevensons. He was such a sickly little boy that they wanted to protect him. But it made him look babyish to the other children. And that made Lou unhappy.

The children made fun of him for being different. They did not let him into their games. Some of the boys bullied him. They punched him, pushed him, and knocked him to the ground.

Lou did not fight back. But he soon found ways to make friends. He learned the games the others played. He learned to talk like the others. Most of all, he used his imagination to make up new games. The children enjoyed his games and soon accepted Lou as one of them. Now school was fun.

Lou was not the best student in the class. He was not good at arithmetic and science. But he learned to read in just a short time, and he loved books. He read everything he could get. He liked fine literature. He also liked the exciting adventure stories that were printed in newspapers. Every week there was a new chapter to read.

Sickness ended Lou's school days for a while. But this time it wasn't Lou who was sick. It was his mother. The family doctor said that Edinburgh was not a good place for her. It was too rainy and cold. The doctor told the Stevensons that a warm, sunny place was best for her. So the family took a trip to the southern part of France. It was very pretty there, but Lou missed school and his classmates.

Lou's parents hired tutors to continue his education. Reading, writing, and drawing were fun for him, so he did them well. But arithmetic and science were torture. He did poorly in those subjects. This didn't please Lou's father. All the Stevensons were engineers. Arithmetic and science were very important in their work. Mr. Stevenson expected Lou to become an engineer when he grew up and join the family business.

The Stevensons returned to Edinburgh when Lou's mother was feeling better. Lou went back to school at Edinburgh Academy, a private school for boys. He was ten years old, but he was short and thin, so he looked younger.

Even though he was not big or athletic, Lou
liked to play some sports. The things he enjoyed
most were swimming, canoeing, hiking, and
horseback riding. He did not enjoy very
competitive or rough sports. He stayed out of
games like Rugby football. It hurt to get knocked
to the ground and kicked around by boys twice
his size.

Lou did take part in a game called Hailes. Hailes was a tradition at Edinburgh Academy. It was played a bit like field hockey. Players held wooden bats called clackans. A clackan was shaped like a long-handled cooking spoon. The ball was caught in the clackan's bowl-shaped end. Then it was passed downfield from player to player. Hailes was mostly a running and passing game. It depended more on skill and speed than on size and strength.

These years were the best of Lou's childhood. He felt healthy and his life was normal. He went to school from Monday through Friday. Saturday and Sunday and vacations were spent with his family.

Lou had many cousins who lived nearby. The children got together as often as they could at Colinton Manse. This was the home of Mrs. Stevenson's parents. Colinton was a large stone house a few miles outside Edinburgh.

At Colinton, there was a lot of land for the children to play on. A swing hung from a large tree, and there were stone walls to climb and walk along. Thick hedges made wonderful hiding places. And there was an old graveyard near the big house.

31

Lou called the path near the garden wall "the Witch's Walk." On the other side of the wall, the river Leith wove its way around the property. The river turned a mill wheel day and night. The children liked to watch the wheel while they played on the river banks. When Lou was an adult, he wrote in a poem, "Keepsake Mill":

"Years may go by, and the wheel in the river
Wheel as it wheels for us, children, today,
Wheel and keep roaring and foaming for ever
Long after all of the boys are away.

Home from the Indies and home from the
　ocean,
Heroes and soldiers we all shall come home;
Still we shall find the old mill wheel in motion,
Turning and churning that river to foam."

Many of Lou's childhood memories are present in his writings, especially in his poetry. *A Child's Garden of Verses* is filled with word-pictures of his young years.

Lou's best friend in those days was his cousin, Robert "Bob" Stevenson. Bob was three years older than Lou, and Lou looked up to him like a big brother. Together the boys made up dozens of games and stories. They invented places called Nosingtonia and Encyclopaedia. These were make-believe islands with their own history and geography. The boys drew maps of their islands. They even created the language spoken by the natives who lived there.

This friendship with Bob was very important to Lou. With Bob sharing in his imagining, no idea was too wild to write about. When he grew up, Robert Louis Stevenson wrote the fabulous novel about the good Dr. Jekyll and the evil Mr. Hyde. These characters were born in Lou's boyhood talks with Cousin Bob. Long John Silver and the tale of *Treasure Island* also began in those long-ago childhood days.

Lou felt lucky to have a friend like Bob. They shared secrets, good and bad feelings, pranks, and jokes. At times, Lou was sick and had to stay in bed for weeks. Even then, Bob came to see him often. Bob was the one friend Lou could always count on.

By the time Lou was a teenager, he wanted to break away from the life he was leading. He wanted to do many things in spite of his medical problems. This troubled his parents. They didn't want Lou to stay out late or to tire himself in any way. He had to wear hats and gloves, sweaters and coats whenever he was out. He had almost no choice in what he did or where he went.

The Stevensons wanted Lou to follow a safe, secure path. They wanted him to be an engineer, just as all the other Stevenson men had been. His family wanted Lou to live with them and let them take care of him.

For a while, Lou tried to do what his parents wanted. He entered Edinburgh University as a student of engineering. But he hated it and did not do well in his classes. Instead, he set out to learn about the people and the city of Edinburgh.

Every day, Lou left his house right after breakfast. His parents thought he was going to school, but he wasn't. He spent hours talking to strangers in shops and to sailors from the ships docked on the Leith. He sat in courtrooms and listened to criminal trials.

38

Some afternoons, Lou went to the theater. He listened to concerts and lectures on many subjects. Best of all, he spent hours and hours with other college students, laughing and talking about everything under the sun. It was an education in life, and he loved it.

When Mr. and Mrs. Stevenson learned what Lou was doing, they were quite upset. They asked their son why he was wasting his time instead of going to class. He said, "I am not wasting time. I do not want to be an engineer. Going to school for that is a true waste of my time. I have decided to be a writer. And the way I have been spending my days is the best education a writer could ask for."

The Stevensons sadly accepted their son's decision not to be an engineer. But they did not want him to become a writer. They felt that writing was not a respectable profession. They suggested that he study law. He objected at first, but finally he agreed.

Lou tried law school for a while, but soon stopped going to classes. He did not like law school. Even more than that, he did not like living at home. His parents still treated him like a sick child, and Lou wanted to come and go as he pleased.

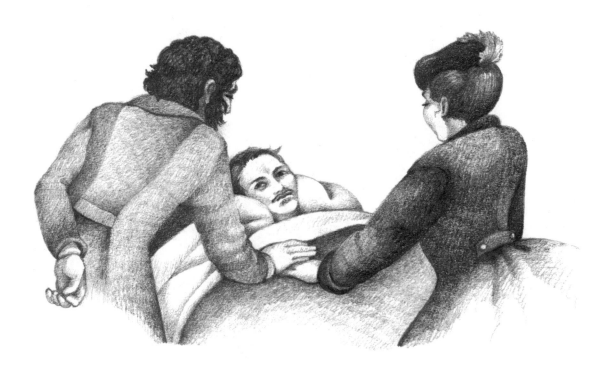

Before long, there was a big family argument. Lou said he wanted to leave home. The Stevensons insisted he continue to study law. At last Lou said he would, but on one condition—if he went to law school in London. That way, he would not be under his parents' rule. Lou's parents accepted this plan.

Lou went to London to take his law-school tests. But when he got there, he fell ill again. The Stevensons rushed to be with him. They planned to take him home as soon as he was able to travel. Lou was very unhappy. Going home was the last thing he wanted to do.

Then, something lucky happened to Lou. He was being treated by a doctor named Andrew Clark. Dr. Clark asked the young man why he was so gloomy. Lou explained everything, and the doctor said he would help solve Lou's problems. Dr. Clark told the Stevensons that Lou needed rest, good food, a warm climate, and time away from his family. He told them that Lou needed to learn to take care of himself. And, Dr. Clark added, a cure often came with independence.

Dr. Andrew Clark was famous and highly respected. So the Stevensons took his advice and went home without their son. A short time later, a cheerful Robert Louis Stevenson sailed for France. It was the beginning of his new life and a memorable career as a writer.

For the next twenty years, Robert Louis Stevenson lived the way he wanted to. He traveled far and wide. He spent many months in the United States. In 1880 he married an American woman, Fanny Osborne. His fame as an author grew every year.

Along with the stories of Jekyll and Hyde and Treasure Island, Stevenson wrote *Kidnapped, The Black Arrow, The Master of Ballantrae, David Balfour,* and other novels, short stories, essays, and poems.

Lou and Fanny and Fanny's son, Lloyd, lived
in Switzerland, Scotland, France, England, and
the United States. Lou had spent so many of his
young years in a sickbed in chilly, rainy
Edinburgh. Now he was free to go where he
wanted, when he wanted. It was better than
anything he'd ever dreamed of.

In 1888, seeking more adventures and new places, Robert Louis Stevenson took his family to the South Seas. They sailed from San Francisco to Tahiti, Hawaii, the Gilbert Islands, and other South Sea ports. They finally settled in Samoa, where Lou continued to write until his death on December 3, 1894. He had come a long way from that lonely little boy who dreamed of lands of make-believe! Robert Louis Stevenson made his dreams come true.